Taj Mahal
Agra and Fatehpur Sikri

Published 2006 by
Prakash Books India Pvt. Ltd.
1, Ansari Road, Daryaganj, New Delhi 110 002, India
sales@prakashbooks.com, www.prakashbooks.com
Tel.: 011-23247062-65

Author: **Subhadra Sen Gupta**
Design: **Saket Misra**

ISBN: 81-7234-130-X

Printed & bound in India at Brijbasi Art Press Ltd., New Delhi

Taj Mahal
Agra and Fatehpur Sikri

Subhadra Sen Gupta

PRAKASH BOOKS

contents

The Great Mughals

In True Imperial Splendour

I f ever a city was the creation of its kings, that city is Agra. The character of any city is a subtle blend of many an element – the landscape, climate, its buildings; its people and their history, heritage and culture; and for some, the kings who ruled from it. With Agra, the most distinctive influence on its personality has been the dynasty of magnificent kings, who chose to make it their capital. From Babur, the founder of the Mughal dynasty in India, to the reigns of his grandson, Akbar, and the two monarchs who followed, Jahangir and Shah Jahan, Agra reached the zenith of its days of splendour. Then, as the power of the Mughals slowly waned and they slid into fratricidal strife and confusion, the glories of Agra also dimmed – like a piece of crystal that glitters and gleams in the morning light but is just a shard of glass at dusk. Once the Mughals abandoned the city, Agra's magnificence never revived. The city went into hibernation carrying the memories of its days of glory in its heart, living with examples in its innumerable monuments. If you want to experience what Mughal India was like, you only have to walk around this city, for the air still carries a flavour of the city's glorious past.

Across the landscape of Agra, among the narrow lanes and serpentine bazaars, stand some of the most unforgettable examples of Mughal architecture. The Mughals were not only enthusiastic builders but were also men of impeccable, aesthetic taste and an adventurous, creative spirit. The edifices they raised are exquisite buildings that evoke an age of true grandeur. The Mughals may have vanished from the polity of India but their presence lingers on in their monuments, ensuring that the land they once ruled will never forget them. As long as Agra stands, the Mughals will be remembered.

For a dynasty that traced its beginnings to two bloodthirsty conquerors, the Mughals evolved into surprisingly cultured and civilised rulers. Compared with most of their contemporaries across the globe, they proved to be enlightened monarchs. To trace their evolution as emperors, one must begin with the extraordinary man – Zahiruddin Muhammad, called Babur, the tiger.

Babur was born in 1483 in the ruling family of Farghana, a tiny principality east of Samarkand, in Afghanistan. His inheritance was not too big but his antecedents were remarkable. He could trace his ancestry back to two of the greatest conquerors in Asia – Timur and Chengiz Khan. Babur himself was more interested in claiming descent from the more cultured Turkish line of Timur and would have been quite disappointed to discover that, centuries later, the dynasty he founded was known across the world for the Mongol marauder, Chengiz Khan.

Babur was only eleven when his father died and he found himself battling to hold on to his inheritance among a group of petty rulers. But ambitious young Babur had no intention of staying on in Farghana. He dreamed of being a conqueror and he had his eye

*previous page: Miniature painting of Babur supervising the building of a pleasure garden. A lover of nature, he built gardens in Kabul and Delhi
courtesy: National Museum*
*left: Miniature paintings of the Mughal School
courtesy: National Museum*
*facing page: From the folio of the Baburnama, by the artist Bhag, 1598
courtesy: National Museum*

on the magnificent capital of Timur – Samarkand. In the following years, in his attempt to conquer this legendary city, the young Babur would lose Farghana too and wander across Central Asia – a nomadic soldier leading raids like a robber just to survive. It was only in 1504 that he found a safe haven for himself and his ragtag band of soldiers when he conquered Kabul. From then on Kabul was to remain his centre of operations from where he would venture out to raid, capture and conquer. It was from here that he turned to look east and began to entertain thoughts about India.

In the early years of the sixteenth century, northern India was ruled from Delhi and Agra by the Lodi kings. In Kabul, Babur had heard of the legendary wealth of the land and seen the traders' caravans coming through the mountain passes of the Hindukush, laden with cloth, spices and jewels. He had also heard of the internal strife within the Lodi court, the weakness of the ruling monarch Ibrahim Lodi, and realised that India was like a ripe fruit that would be easy to pluck, just as his ancestor Timur had done long ago. After a few exploratory forays across the borders of Punjab to raid and retreat, he finally launched a proper expedition to India in 1526.

The two armies of Sultan Ibrahim Lodi and Babur met on the fields of Panipat. Babur's army had twenty-five thousand men, but the Sultan's forces were nearly four times as many and had an immense phalanx of a thousand elephants. However, what he lacked in numbers, Babur made up in strategy, courage and the clever use of his musketeers. The guns scared the elephants into rampaging, while groups of horsemen led by Babur's

*Pavilion and water channel at Arambagh, Agra,
the first Mughal garden laid out by Humayun*

seventeen-year-old son Humayun wheeled behind the Lodi army and routed the enemy. By the end of the day, Ibrahim Lodi was dead and Babur marched into Delhi in triumph.

Babur stayed on in Delhi while the *qutba* (an official declaration by the clergy of the state) was read in the mosques declaring him the new king, but sent Humayun with a small detachment of horses on a fast foray to Agra to capture the Lodi treasury. The first Mughal to enter Agra was the young Humayun. Here he discovered that the Gwalior family had taken refuge in the old fort and asked for his protection as the *raja* had died at Panipat. Among the gifts presented by the royal family to Humayun was a magnificent diamond that he presented to his father, when Babur arrived a few days later. This was the legendary *Kohinoor*. "Humayun offered it to me when I arrived in Agra," wrote Babur in his memoirs, "I just gave it back to him."

Babur was not just the founder of the Mughal dynasty in India, he also set the tenor of its rule and the traditions of kingship. He was a man of varied talents and in spite of the nomadic and conflict-ridden life that he led, he had developed a cultural bent of mind and great aesthetic qualities. Babur was a poet; he wrote a meticulously honest memoir that not only chronicled his life but also created a detailed portrait of the land that he had conquered. He took great pleasure in studying the flora and fauna of this new land, filling the pages with miniature paintings by the court artists, though his first impression of India was far from a happy one. For a man coming from the cool air and hilly orchards of Kabul, Agra in the month of May could hardly have been pleasant. He was to write in the *Baburnama*, "There are no good horses, no good dogs, no grapes, musk melons or first-rate fruits, no ice or cold water." Still he chose to stay and set standards of kingship that became a tradition with most of his descendants. An enlightened tradition of tolerance and a lack of religious bigotry were coupled with a preference for aesthetics in painting, garden landscaping and buildings, music, poetry and even a taste for stylish opulence.

Timur had only come to raid India; Babur chose to build an empire here. He made Agra his capital and as was his style, began his reign by creating elegant gardens in Panipat and at Agra, giving them poetic names to match – Zar Afshan (a scattering of gold) and Gul Afshan (a scattering of flowers). Here he completed his memoirs, the *Baburnama*, a surprisingly frank and thoughtful chronicle. However, all Babur could really do was create an outpost of his kingdom at Agra when, just four years later, he died in 1530. A generous, liberal man who travelled with a camel-load of books, Babur would one day get a fitting descendent in his grandson, Akbar.

Babur's eldest son, Humayun now became the king. He was brave in battle, liberal in spirit, but also a weak and sentimental man who lacked judgement. Babur had only conquered the land; what was needed now was a king who could establish a kingdom. All Humayun did instead was spend his days trying to control his two troublesome brothers, who were forever conspiring to capture the throne. A man who couldn't rein in his own brothers was hardly capable of holding on to a fledgling kingdom still full of rebellious men from an earlier regime.

Humayun chose to make Delhi his capital, laying the foundation of a new city he called Dinpanah. Only the outer walls of the new capital had come up when a new threat emerged from the east. Humayun marched out to face a rebel who possessed the talent and temperament to defeat him. Sher Khan was an Afghan soldier of fortune who had succeeded in collecting all the Lodi supporters behind him and, after raiding Bengal, was now marching swiftly towards Delhi. Humayun was trapped between Sher Khan before him and his treacherous brothers behind him and had neither the shrewdness nor the courage to extricate himself from this impasse.

After successive defeats, Humayun retreated to Lahore. Sher Khan captured Delhi and declared himself king from the city that Humayun had started to build. Now, as Sher Shah Suri, he built his own palaces there and began to rule. It looked like the old line of Sultans had returned to power and Babur's dream of an Indian kingdom had faded within a single generation.

Like his father had once done, Humayun now wandered around Afghanistan without a home. His brothers, one ruling at Lahore and the other at Kabul, did not welcome him in their kingdoms. It was during this nomadic existence that a son was born to him in 1542, at Umarkot. Humayun named him Akbar. It was in 1545 that Humayun's fortunes changed when, with the help of Shah Tahmasp of Persia, he put together an army. He regained Kabul from his brother Kamran and with conditions in India being favourable, he planned to march on to Delhi. The Suri empire had disintegrated after the death of Sher Shah and, with his faithful general Bairam Khan by his side, Humayun returned to Delhi in triumph, in 1555.

A scholar like his father, Humayun turned one of the palaces of Sher Shah into his library. He also brought two miniature painters from Persia, Mir Sayyid Ali and Khwaja Abdus Samad, who would one day establish a school of miniature painting in India. However, Humayun had few days left to enjoy his return to power. In 1556, he stumbled down the staircase of his library and died of injuries. Young Akbar was now declared king at the tender age of thirteen. Few would have given him a chance for survival with at least three Afghan claimants to the throne. Fortunately, Akbar had general Bairam Khan by his side.

The crucial battle that established Akbar's right to the throne was again fought at Panipat in 1556. Here he defeated the army of his most dangerous challenger, Hemu, the Hindu minister of one of the Afghan claimants who had grown ambitious after a succession of victories. Again the opposition had the larger army but Hemu was injured by an arrow and his soldiers fled thinking he was dead. The victorious Akbar was now the undisputed king of Hindustan. As he had done for Humayun, it was Bairam Khan's courage and sagacity that had brought him success. Later it would be this old general's careful administration that would make the kingdom safe.

Like his grandfather, Akbar chose to make Agra his capital with Delhi as an important centre of the empire. He arrived in Agra in 1558, floating down the river Yamuna in a luxurious royal barge with a flotilla of decorated courtiers' boats in attendance. He embarked at the old fort of Badalgarh after a leisurely three-week cruise. For the next hundred years, Agra would be the heart of the Mughal Empire, that is till 1658, when Akbar's grandson, Shah Jahan, would shift the capital to Delhi again. These were the years of splendour for Agra when the opulent royal court was the destination of soldiers and poets, musicians and traders, when the bazaars buzzed with commerce, the shops overflowing with goods from far-off lands. Forts, luxurious palaces and the *havelis* of courtiers rose everywhere; gardens and mosques were built by royals and noblemen.

Few looking at young Akbar, as he began his reign, would have believed that he would succeed in laying the foundations on which the monolith of the empire would rest. For a clan that took pride in its education and where even the ladies of the harem were often scholars and poets, he didn't seem interested in studies and would remain the

top: The Anup Talao, where musicians
performed for Akbar, Fatehpur Sikri
above: Details of carvings in red sandstone, Fatehpur Sikri

only Mughal who was barely literate. He spent his days hunting, riding and taming wild animals, showing not the least interest in learning the art of kingship, leaving all the work of statesmanship to Bairam Khan.

And yet, Akbar was fated to become the greatest monarch of the dynasty. One day this same youth would evolve into a man deeply interested in books, paintings and craftsmanship. He would also become ambitious, leading successful expeditions until the borders of his empire stretched nearly over the whole of India, from Kabul and Kashmir in the North to Khandesh in the South, touching Gujarat in the West and including Bengal in the East. A military genius with great talent of leadership, he never lost a battle. His reign built the foundations of an empire that lasted three centuries.

Akbar was the first Islamic monarch to realise that mere occupation does not create an empire. What he aimed to create was not an Islamic or Timurid empire but one with an

above: The marble tomb of Sufi saint Sheikh
Salim Chishti, in the courtyard of the
Jami Masjid, Fatehpur Sikri
following page: Akbar supervises building
of Fatehpur Sikri. Mughal miniature from the
Akbarnama
courtesy: Victoria & Albert Museum, London

Indian ethos. He set about with great energy to win the loyalties of the Hindu populace and for his special attention he chose the Rajput princes whose opposition could end his ambitions, and whose loyalty could give it a brave army of soldiers. At twenty, he married the daughter of the Raja of Amber. Muslim rulers had married Hindu princesses before him but what made this alliance unique was that the princess was allowed to remain a Hindu and practice her religion freely. Other such marriages followed and the royal court soon became cosmopolitan with many Hindu kings in high positions of power and even within the emperor's circle of trusted advisers, such as Raja Man Singh and Raja Birbal. He not only succeeded in projecting himself as an Indian king but also gained the loyalty of his court through his administrative shrewdness. His revenue system, for example, would be followed for centuries after – the pioneering work of his revenue minister, Raja Todar Mal.

For a man of his times, Akbar was surprisingly liberal and curious when it came to matters of religion, with a mystic bent of mind. He cancelled two unpopular religious taxes that Hindus had to pay, in spite of the opposition of the clergy. He celebrated the festivals of all faiths and would one day unveil a religion of his own that was an idealistic blend of the elements that he had liked in all the religions he had encountered. As Abul Fazl, his biographer, explained it, the king's background predetermined his open-mindedness as he was "the child of a Sunni father and a Shia mother, born in Hindustan, in the land of Sufism, at the house of a Hindu." Though his new faith, *Din-i-Ilahi*, did not last beyond the reign of its creator, the fact remains that no religious group could ever be certain that Akbar was on their side, and this led to an age of surprising religious tolerance and moderation that gave the country the breathing space it needed to recover from years of tyranny.

At twenty-six, Akbar was at the height of his power but to his sorrow he had no living heir. In 1568, a Sufi saint, Sheikh Salim Chishti, who lived near a village called Sikri, assured him of the birth of three sons. The following year, the princess of Amber bore him a son who was named Salim after the saint. Kings have been known to build palaces and mosques in gratitude, but Akbar chose to build an entire city. He had long wanted to shift out of Agra's fort to a new capital and now decided to build it at Sikri. Work began on the palaces in 1571, and the new city that the emperor called Fatehpur Sikri was ready within fourteen years. The royal court shifted here and it was an age of great pomp and grandeur. Arts and crafts, music and literature – all flourished under the king's personal attention. At the *karkhanas* or ateliers of Sikri, miniature painters and carpet weavers, sculptors and wood carvers worked. Singers like Mian Tansen and Baz Bahadur were among the jewels of the court. Scholars led by Abul Fazl, his brother Faizi the poet, and Abdur Rahim Khan-i-Khanan created classics. But fifteen years later, Akbar moved his capital abruptly back to Agra for which many reasons have been attributed like shortage of water, but the chronicles of the time are surprisingly quiet on the subject.

Once, writing to his son Murad, Akbar spoke of the duties of a good king: "Let not difference of religion interfere with policy, and be not violent in inflicting retribution. Adorn the confidential council with men who know their work. If apologies be made, accept them." If any king deserved the appellation of 'great', Akbar did. When he died in 1605, he left behind a peaceful and prosperous empire that was already on its way to becoming a legend across the world for its wealth and magnificence. His son Salim succeeded him to the throne of Hindustan, taking the title of 'Jahangir' (Seizer of the World).

نور جهان

facing page: Miniature portrait of Nurjahan Begum.
The Empress who had coins struck in her own name
courtesy: National Museum
above: *Miniature portrait of Emperor Jahangir, holding*
a portrait of the Virgin Mary
courtesy: National Museum
following page: *Gateway to Akbar's tomb, Sikandra*

Jahangir lacked Akbar's energy and ambition; instead, his interest lay more in paintings, cultural and scientific matters. He did not relish leading military expeditions and was hardly inclined to run an empire. Fortunately for him, Akbar had left behind a peaceful and well-run kingdom with few pockets of opposition. Jahangir left most of his work of administration to his advisers. Within a few years of his reign, the sceptre of power moved into the hands of a woman, the empress Nur Jahan. The empress and her family wielded enormous influence. Her father was her main adviser and her brother Asaf Khan rose in eminence when Jahangir's son Khurram (from an earlier wife) married his daughter Arjumand Bano.

If the Mughal Empire survived Jahangir's intermittent interest and frequent apathy, it was because of the energetic efficiency of Nur Jahan, formerly known as Mehrunnissa, the daughter of a Persian courtier in Akbar's court, Mirza Ghiyas Beg. She was married first to a soldier, Sher Afgan, and lived in Bengal. At her husband's death she returned to Agra where, as a lady-in-waiting in the harem, she caught the eye of Jahangir who married her and gave her the title Nur Jahan (Light of the World). An intelligent, strong-willed and capable woman, she succeeded in ruling from behind the screens of the harem, with Asaf Khan ensuring that her wishes were carried out. She heard petitions, meted out justice and gave final approval to any royal decree. The women of the harem were often influential at court but none of them possessed the courage and dynamism of Nur Jahan.

It was Nur Jahan who gave Agra its most elegant building, the mausoleum she built for her father Ghiyas Beg – the tomb of Itmad-ud-Daula, an exquisitely finished jewel-box of a structure that possesses the delicacy of design to rival the Taj Mahal. Jahangir, like his grandfather Babur, kept a diary – *Tuzuk-i-Jahangiri* – and it is a detailed and honest chronicle.

Unlike Akbar, Jahangir was not a keen builder. During his reign, only two royal structures were built – Akbar's tomb at Sikandra, and Itmad-ud-Daula's memorial. But as a connoisseur of fine arts, his thrust was on miniature painting. Akbar had used his school of painters to illustrate manuscripts and paint important episodes of his reign. Jahangir encouraged his painters to do studies from nature, and portraits. Paintings from this era possess an exquisite precision of detail and fine craftsmanship. He also loved laying out gardens, most of which he created in his beloved Kashmir.

In the last years of his reign, Jahangir was saddened by a battle for power between his wife and his most capable son, Khurram. When he died in 1627, matters were settled in Khurram's favour when Asaf Khan chose to back his son-in-law instead of his sister. Khurram came to the throne in 1628, took the title of Shah Jahan, and his queen Arjumand Bano now came to be known as Mumtaz Mahal. Khurram's path to power was a bloody one with two brothers, several nephews and cousins losing their lives in the battle to the throne of Agra. Shah Jahan, of course, could not look into the future or he would have seen the same tragedy being enacted again among his own sons while he would have to watch as a helpless spectator. The source of trouble lay in the fact that the Mughals had no tradition of succession, with the eldest son automatically ascending to the throne. At the end of each reign, therefore, a fratricidal battle became inevitable.

Shah Jahan gave Agra and the world the immortal Taj Mahal, but the story of this monument begins with the greatest tragedy of his life. In the early years of his reign, his beloved confidante and empress, Mumtaz Mahal died at childbirth. She had accompanied him on a military expedition as was her wont, and died at Burhanpur. She was then only

thirty-nine. After her death, Shah Jahan lost interest in the work of the state and in empire-building. Leaving all military expeditions and the governance of the provinces to his sons and advisers, he now concentrated on his biggest passion – architecture.

All his life Shah Jahan had exhibited a love for building and this came with an imaginative ability to visualise the structure in detail and then touch it with Mughal opulence. By the time of his reign, the empire was known to be one of the richest in the world, its treasury full of gems and jewels, leaving him with the means to satisfy even the grandest of whims. With him began the Mughals' romance with marble. Akbar had chosen the austere red sandstone, his grandson preferred the richness of marble decorated with the finest inlay of semi-precious stones. By the end of his reign, he is said to have exhausted the vast resources of the royal treasury but, in return, he created some truly magnificent buildings, the best being the incomparable Taj Mahal and the palaces, forts, mosques and bazaars of his capital city of Shahjahanabad, in Delhi.

The royal court was one of the grandest India had ever seen. Traders carried stories across continents about the grandeur of the 'Great Mogul' and Europeans flocked to Agra begging to do business with India. Looking at all the pomp and panoply of the empire, few could have believed that Shah Jahan and his sons were then even sowing the seeds of the destruction of their dynasty.

The traditional royal policy of religious tolerance that Akbar had begun was now often ignored. Shah Jahan, in spite of being three-quarters Hindu, lacked his grandfather's enlightened approach to kingship. If the kingdom did not revert to its earlier Islamic bigotry, it was only because of the beneficial influence of his eldest son, Dara Shikoh.

Then Shah Jahan's extravagant building work began to deplete the treasury. He first built the Taj and then a new city at Delhi at enormous expense, and then indulged himself with the Peacock Throne, a fabulous jewel-encrusted throne that used up a large part of the gems in the royal treasury. The emperor's love for grand spectacle and his endless hubris made him blind to what his extravagance was doing to the empire.

There was little love lost between Shah Jahan's four sons. As the emperor aged, the sons prepared themselves for the inevitable war of succession. In 1657, Shah Jahan fell ill and it was feared he would die. Dara Shikoh was beside the emperor but his three brothers, governors of different provinces, marched towards Delhi on the pretext of visiting their ailing father. A battle ensued between his two ablest sons, Aurangzeb and Dara Shikoh. A shrewd strategist and tough military general, Aurangzeb had the will and tenacity that the cultured and liberal Dara Shikoh did not possess. As the emperor watched helplessly, Aurangzeb triumphed after a bloody conflict in which only he survived. He declared himself emperor in 1658, and imprisoned his father at Agra Fort.

The centre of power now shifted to Delhi from where Aurangzeb ruled. The later Mughal kings too remained there. The days of Agra's glory were drawing to a close. A last glimmer of passing splendour lay with the man who had given this city its most beautiful building – the aging Shah Jahan counting his last days watching the Taj Mahal from the verandah of the Mussaman Burj at the Fort. He would survive in captivity for eight long years, tended faithfully by his daughter, Jahanara. Then in 1666, Shah Jahan died and was buried next to his beloved Mumtaz Mahal and with him vanished the days of Agra's grandeur.

previous page: Miniature portraits of
Mumtaz Mahal and Shahjahan. Her untimely
death would inspire Shahjahan to build the
magnificent Taj Mahal
facing page: The Mussaman Burj, the
Jasmine Tower, Agra Fort. Shahjahan spent his
last days here, gazing at the Taj Mahal
above: Details of pietra-dura inlay on marble
with semi-precious stones

Akbar's Agra
A Serenade in Sandstone

THE FORT

With the arrival of Akbar, the history of Agra as a capital city begins because it was he, more than any other Mughal monarch, who gave Agra its imperial character. Babur gave the Mughals their foothold in India and Humayun barely held on to what had been gained, but with Akbar the centre of power moved to Agra for over a century. As Abul Fazl, the royal historian wrote about Akbar's decision to build a fort in Agra in 1565, "Accordingly, he at this time gave directions for the building in Agra – which by its position in the centre of Hindustan – of a grand fortress such as might be worthy thereof, and correspond to the dignity of the dominions...completed with all its battlements, breastwork and its loopholes, in the space of eight years under the faithful superintendence of Qasim Khan, Mir Barr-u-Bahr." From then, on for many years,

above: The forbidding bastions of the Agra Fort
following page, left: The imposing Amarsingh Gate, the second portal of the Agra Fort
following page, right: The third gate beyond the Amarsingh Gate. Drummers sat in the gallery above, the Nakkar Khana, and played to welcome royal personages

the city was named after the king. Jahangir, for instance, always referred to it as Akbarabad. It was just that – first and foremost, it was Akbar's city.

For a true introduction to the Mughals who ruled from Agra, you must begin at the Fort. It is here that the transition from Akbar to Jahangir and then to Shah Jahan is still preserved in its battlements, palaces and gates. Each monarch added to the structure that was originally built by Akbar. In the eyes of the historian it still remains the gateway to the city.

When Akbar began his reign, his hold over his kingdom was still fragile and he needed a fort that could be defended against an invading army. He chose a site by the banks of the Yamuna, at a curve of the river where the water acted as an additional moat, and built his first fort which was also his first architectural venture. Nearly four thousand labourers worked at the site and many chroniclers mention Akbar being personally present to supervise them. As a Jesuit in Akbar's court, Monserrate, watching him at Sikri, wrote, "Zelaldinus [Jalal-ud-din Akbar's name] is so devoted to building that he sometimes quarries himself along with other workmen. Nor does he shrink from watching, and even practicing, for the sake of amusement, the craft of an ordinary artisan." The immense enterprise was completed in just eight years.

High, red sandstone walls rose up to twenty-two metres in height with a deep moat between two layers of protective walls. The fort was built in a crescent shape following the curve of the river, and the double walls that encircled it were pierced by slits for the musketeers. The walls with battlements, embrasures and drawbridges over the moat were pierced by four gates. Two, the Hathi Pol and the Amar Singh Gate, are still open with Naqqar Khanas or drum houses over them. Few, looking at the curved walls and turrets that stretch for a distance of over a kilometre, would be able to imagine the exquisite palaces and mosques, the marble fountains and gardens within. The Fort at Agra established the model for all Mughal forts that were built after it – Akbar himself would build two more at Lahore and Allahabad, which were conceived in the same pattern. Even the last Mughal fort to be built, the Red Fort in Delhi which Shah Jahan, an acknowledged architectural expert, designed, sticks to the same basic format.

When he was building his fort, Akbar, of course, was not to know that one day he would have a grandson who would be an obsessive builder. Shah Jahan remodelled and rebuilt extensive portions of the Fort, but during later British rule large portions were callously destroyed and replaced with army barracks. This is something the British also did at the Red Fort in Delhi where most of the palaces of the harem and a whole road of elegant *havelis* were razed in a vindictive act of revenge for the Indian uprising of 1857, though it was claimed to have been done for reasons of security. In Delhi, at least the important buildings remained but in Agra Fort, between the remodelling of Shah Jahan and the handiwork of the British, little of what Akbar built remains in its original shape.

One of the few palaces that still shows the unique Akbari style is Jahangiri Mahal that he is said to have built for his son. This is the earliest example of Akbar's beautiful blend of Indian and Islamic architectural traditions. Most of his craftsmen, the stone-cutters and inlay workers, were Indian and Akbar, to his credit, did not force them to create in an unfamiliar style, instead allowing them to develop an exquisite mix. For instance, two *mahals* or palaces mentioned in the chronicles of the time are Bengali Mahal, where Akbar's queen and Jahangir's mother, the princess of Amber, probably lived, and another built in the style of Gujarat.

The craftsmanship was of the highest order and even astounded visitors from other lands,

above: Details of the Jahangiri Mahal, Agra Fort
following page: The Jahangiri Mahal, Agra Fort
page no. 38: Inside courtyard of the Jahangiri Mahal, Agra Fort
page no. 39: Exterior of the Diwan-i-Khas, the Hall of Private Audiences, Agra Fort

as Monserrate had marvelled in 1580, "The stones of these buildings are so cunningly fitted that the joints are scarcely visible, although no lime was used to fix them together. The beautiful colour of the stone, which is all red, also produces the same effect of uniform solidity." Like all Mughal forts, this was first a palace with the monarch's personal quarters and the harem; then it was the administrative heart of the empire with offices and army barracks; and finally it was a citadel. It was also the treasure house where the growing Mughal treasury was kept. The historian Badauni notes, "After it was completed it became the depository and store house of all the gold of Hindustan." Through the centuries it faced much plunder and pillage. The Jats took away most of the pietra-dura inlay done in semi-precious stones and even the marble tanks and reservoirs from the Machhi Bhavan to put in their palaces in Deeg. The British dispatched carved marble baths to England to please the Prince Regent and even auctioned some marble pieces in 1830.

At the entrance of Jahangiri Mahal is a huge hall that leads off into a courtyard surrounded by columns. The ceilings are supported by stone beams carved like undulating serpents – the style of wooden roof beams recreated in stone. The rooms have finely carved columns and nichés and probably some of them were used by Jahangir's empress, Nur Jahan. Carved stone lattices screened off the passageways that were used by the women. There is also a beautiful open porch that overlooks the river with the red sandstone walls decorated with highlights of marble.

Jahangir himself did little building in the fort, at least what still remains is the handiwork of Shah Jahan. Where Akbar had built in sandstone, Shah Jahan had now added marble, even remodelling one wing of Jahangiri Mahal and adding a tower with a pavilion. His concentration was taken up with the building of his lavish personal quarters, Khas Mahal. Built in 1637, the sandstone and marble pavilions overlook the river with elegant arches,

fountains and tapering turrets on the roof. The walls were once decorated with delicate inlay in semi-precious stones but successive hordes of invaders have removed most of them. The *mahal* has underground rooms which were used by the occupants during the scorching heat of summer. After he was dethroned and imprisoned by his son in the Fort, Shah Jahan only had the company of his eldest daughter during the last eight years of his life, and the Princess Jahanara stayed at the Khas Mahal. The garden before the Khas Mahal is called Anguri Bagh or Garden of Grapes though there are no remains of a vineyard here. It resembles the typical Mughal garden with its geometric design, water channels and fountains.

In the Fort are some of the earliest examples of a Sheesh Mahal or Palace of Mirrors. Many later Mughal palaces also have them. Here, the Sheesh Mahal was the royal bath and dressing room for the harem. As the fragments of glass catch every passing movement, it is easy to imagine the small mirrors embedded in the wall reflecting the flash of a bejewelled arm, the curving rays of the sun during the daytime and the flicker of a moving candle's flame at night. The Mughals, and especially Shah Jahan, were sybarites and the Sheesh Mahals were a part of that opulent lifestyle.

The Diwan-i-Aam presents the public face of the Mughals. It is here, in this superbly proportioned palace, that the monarch met his subjects in the Hall of Public Audience. There is some uncertainty as to the builder of this low, colonnaded building with cusped Mughal arches supported by slender pillars – was it Akbar, Jahangir or Shah Jahan? Unfortunately, most official chronicles of the time do not bother to give details of the building works of the king. But it is certainly Shah Jahan who transformed the throne room with milk white marble and exquisitely graceful inlays. Mulla Abdul Hamid described its "ceiling embossed with gold and made a counterpart of the roof of heaven." It is here that the king would listen to his subjects, pass judgement and receive noblemen. The physician Bernier describes the

previous page: The Diwan-i-Am, the Hall of Public Audiences, Agra Fort
above: The interior of the Diwan-i-Am
facing page, left: The throne in the Diwan-i-Am, Agra Fort
following page: The Bangla Pavilion with the copper domes where the exiled Princess Jahanara stayed, Agra Fort

scene, "The monarch, every day about noon, sits upon his throne with some of his sons at his right and left, while eunuchs, standing about the royal persons, flap away flies with peacock tails, agitate the air with large fans or wait with profound humility to perform the different services allotted to them."

Just beyond the Diwan-i-Khas, there is a courtyard lined by apartments near the Macchi Bhavan, the quaintly named Palace of Fish. It is said the Meena Bazaar used to be held here. At this bazaar the monarch relaxed after a day of tiring royal duties with a bit of flirtation. The bazaar was a part of the harem and in a tradition started by Akbar, the ladies of the harem regularly set up shop there, selling trinkets, silks and jewellery. The only customers were men of the royal family and courtiers with special standing within the royal family. Jahangir met the young Mehrunnissa at this bazaar and was smitten enough to make her his empress: one day she would become the real power behind the throne as Nur Jahan.

The Diwan-i-Khas or the Hall of Private Audience was built by Shah Jahan. For all their lifestyle of pomp and luxury, the Mughals were hardworking monarchs and it was here that the real work of the empire was conducted as the king took care of important matters of state, listening to reports from his ministers, pondering over messages from the provinces and receiving ambassadors from other countries. The lavishly carved marble columns and arches give this hall a light, airy ambience. The palace has two marble thrones, one in white and the other carved out of a single block of black marble. Jahangir is said to have built the black one but Shah Jahan preferred to create his own in his favourite white.

Shah Jahan's tragic last days were spent in Musamman Burj or Jasmine Tower. This delightful, octagonal tower was built by him for his queen Mumtaz Mahal, with carved fountains and latticed screens. The broken Shah Jahan, imprisoned in the Fort, spent his last days in the Burj, looking down the river at the Taj Mahal. They say that as his eyes weakened, he used to look at a reflection of the Taj in the mirror on the wall – the historic, timeless monument that has earned a pride of place as the seventh wonder of the world and comes under the aegis of UNESCO's World Heritage.

There are two mosques within the walls of the Fort. Nagina Masjid with its cusped arches, three graceful domes and a marble courtyard, was built by Shah Jahan for the ladies of the harem. Moti Masjid or Pearl Mosque was also built by him for his personal use. All in marble, this graceful building has cloisters and screens behind which the ladies came to

pray. The three perfectly balanced domes are beautifully offset by elegant Persian arches. It is a small jewel-like building that reminds one of another marble Pearl Mosque at Delhi's Red Fort that Aurangzeb built for his personal worship.

The Fort in Agra, in spite of the ravages of time, retains a flavour of its Mughal past. It is from here that Akbar rode out to conquer the kingdoms of India; Jahangir spent his days bent over exquisite miniature paintings as he sipped from a silver goblet of wine; while Nur Jahan went hunting tigers in a covered howdah. And it was here that Shah Jahan dreamed of a marble memorial to his empress that is today a symbol of not just Agra but of India.

facing page: The Taj Mahal in the distance, as visible from the Mussaman Burj, Agra Fort
above: The lavishly adorned interiors of the Mussaman Burj, Agra Fort
left: Details of marble inlay work inside the Mussaman Burj

FATEHPUR SIKRI

Only an emperor like Akbar could have built a city like Fatehpur Sikri. It is not that the other Mughals did not establish new cities – his father Humayun began construction of one at Jahanpanah in Delhi, his grandson Sha h Jahan would one day give Delhi its seventh and most magnificent metropolis. What made Akbar's act so unique was the reason, even the impulse behind it. The others, when they raised gateways and palaces, were putting the stamp of their power and presence on the landscape. Akbar dreamed of a new capital city out of a sense of gratitude to a penniless Sufi saint.

If it wasn't true, you'd think it was a fairy tale or a fanciful legend. In 1568, Akbar's empire stretched across North India. He was acknowledged as the supreme monarch by all, his court a glittering congregation of royals, nobility, scholars and musicians. The land was prosperous and peaceful. But the Mughal had no living heir. For a man of his ambitions, the absence of a son to follow him on the throne of Hindustan was a shattering and unbearable prospect.

Akbar had visited innumerable holy shrines, consulted astrologers, gone on pilgrimages,

walked barefoot to pray at Ajmer. In his twenty-sixth year, he stopped at a small village called Sikri, forty kilometre outside Agra. There he heard of the Sufi saint who lived in a shack up the hill and Akbar trudged up to pay his respects. The Sufi, Sheikh Salim Chishti, predicted that Akbar would have not one but three sons and, to the king's delight, within a year the prediction came true. Akbar's Hindu queen, the princess of Amber gave birth to a son who was named Salim after the Sufi saint. Within a few years two other sons, Murad and Daniyal were born to other queens.

In 1571, Akbar decided to build a new capital city for which he chose the site where Salim Chishti stayed. As Jahangir corroborates in his memoirs, "My revered father, considering the village of Sikri, which was the place of my birth, lucky for him, made it his capital." It was an act of gratitude that matched Akbar's character. Of course, there were other reasons of polity and kingship, for Akbar was too astute a king to do anything for purely emotional reasons. The Mughal Empire deserved a more impressive capital than the Agra Fort. Akbar was an inveterate builder always looking for an excuse to build, and he felt that the empire was now strong enough not to be barred behind a citadel's barricade of high walls.

So a city came up on the hill at Sikri. In 1571, in his fortieth year, after his yearly pilgrimage

to Ajmer, Akbar halted at Sikri and in the words of the chronicler Abul Fazl, "Now that his standard had arrived at that place, his former design was pressed forward and an order was issued that the superintendents of affairs should erect lofty buildings for the special use of the Shahinshah." The top of the hill was sliced off to create space for the palaces. As at the Agra Fort, Akbar preferred to build in red sandstone and here it was available from the hill itself, and the style was of a refined simplicity that was so typical of Akbar who never chose ostentation over grandeur. Roads curved up the ridge to the complex of palaces, mosques, army barracks, treasury and offices. The court naturally also moved with the king, and the houses of nobles came up around the royal enclosure. Akbar, returning after a triumphant conquest of Gujarat, initially named his new capital Fatehabad, but later it came to be known as Fatehpur, City of Victory.

As always, the emperor took a personal interest in the construction, regularly visiting the site and there are miniature paintings showing him with masons, stone carvers and labourers. In the words of Jahangir, "that hill full of wild beasts became a city containing all kinds of gardens and buildings, lofty edifices and pleasant places attractive to the heart." All the noblemen built their *havelis* up the ridge beside the royal road. Factories, *caravan serais*

previous page: A panoramic view of Fatehpur Sikri
above: A panoramic view of the courtyard and the Diwan-i-Khas, Fatehpur Sikri
following page: Two views of the central pillar with radial passages on top, in the Diwan-i-Khas, Fatehpur Sikri

and bazaars sprang up. Within a few years Fatehpur Sikri was a busy, thriving city.

The Mughal court had its most resplendent years at Fatehpur Sikri. The scholar-historian Abul Fazl wrote the biography of the king, *Akbarnama*; singers like Tansen and Baz Bahadur created new *ragas*, Faizi composed poetry. The royal ateliers were producing miniature paintings, carpets, carvings, and woven cloth. In the evocative words of Monserrate, there were "studios and workrooms for the finer and more reputable arts, such as painting, goldsmith work, tapestry-making, carpet and curtain-making and the manufacture of arms." Fourteen years of occupation later, on his return from an expedition to Lahore, Akbar chose to stay at Agra Fort. The court too moved back, though all chronicles are silent about the reasons.

When Akbar and his court abandoned Fatehpur Sikri, the city went to sleep. The palaces

and open courtyards, the pleasure pavilions and gardens lay waiting for another royal Mughal to touch them with the magic wand of life. No one came. In this city frozen in time are some of the best preserved examples of Mughal architecture. Untouched by other builders, this is truly Akbar's city where except for the ravages of time, very little has changed.

The Jami Masjid or the imperial mosque is one of the most elegant structures at Fatehpur Sikri. Built in red sandstone with exquisite inlay work highlighting the carving, it has a simple but graceful symmetry. Unlike other Mughal mosques like the Jami Masjid in Delhi, it has an intimate and quietly charming air. The open quadrangle for the worshippers is surrounded by arcaded cloisters, high walls and battlements and the courtyard can hold up to ten thousand worshippers. It is the first of the congregational mosques to be built by a Mughal, all earlier ones being for their personal worship, such as those at Agra Fort.

At one end of the courtyard of the Jami Masjid looms the immense gateway of Buland Darwaza. This was built later to celebrate Akbar's victory in Gujarat. After a stepped terrace that rises 42 feet in height, this impressive gateway looms another 134 feet higher over a platform, topped with canopied *chattris* and battlements. Within the archway is an enormous hall and a number of small apartments that lead into the courtyard of the mosque. In spite of its bulk, it is decorated delicately in marble inlay and chaste carvings. The Darwaza is visible for miles into the countryside and art-historian Percy Brown says it "is a work of great force, especially when viewed from the ground below, as then it presents an appearance of aspiring and overwhelming strength without being weighty and pretentious."

As if a counterpoint to the impressive Darwaza, in the centre of the courtyard of Jami Masjid is the delicately beautiful shrine of Sheikh Salim Chishti. The tomb was built in 1571,

facing page: Intricate jali screen at Salim
Chishti's tomb, Fatehpur Sikri
above: The five-storeyed Panch Mahal,
Fatehpur Sikri
following page: The marble tomb of the
Sufi saint Sheikh Salim Chishti that stands in the
courtyard of the Jama Masjid, Fatehpur Sikri

by Nawab Qutub-ud-din Khan, and was probably covered in marble some time during the last days of Jahangir or the early part of the reign of Shah Jahan. The inner sanctum where the saint lies is covered by a canopy in ebony and mother-of-pearl. A corridor surrounds the sanctum and its walls are in a fragile latticework through which sunlight filters in gently. Some of the carvings on the pillars in the portico and the convoluted struts with an intricate, perforated effect are in unusual serpentine motifs and give the impression of marble lace. In all of Fatehpur Sikri, this shrine is the most alive, as women come here to pray for a child. Singers outside raise their voices in praise of the Sufi saint whose holiness permeates the air like a gentle fragrance.

Near one of the main public gates is the Diwan-i-Am, the Hall of Public Audience. It is designed as an open garden or courtyard surrounded by open cloisters and with the hall of judgement at one end. Akbar's throne was placed here and he dispensed justice and listened to petitions from his subjects. Commoners were not allowed beyond this courtyard, as past the walls lay Akbar's private world.

Just behind the Diwan-i-Am is a stone courtyard and in the centre is a chequered square where fanciful people say Akbar played chess with living slave girls as pieces. The

quadrangle has come to be called the Pachisi courtyard. At one corner of the open space stands his Hall of Private Audience, the Diwan-i-Khas. This building, with its unpretentious exterior, is one of the most idiosyncratic structures in the city. Outside, it is a simple, rather plain and austere, square building. Inside, however, is a large, high-ceilinged room in the centre of which looms a thick, carved stone column with a flat-topped pinnacle connected with the galleries on the sides by narrow stone passageways. The capital is square at the base, then octagonal and then flares to sixteen sides on the top, with elaborately carved brackets supporting an elevated seat. It is said that Akbar's throne was placed on top of the platform with the courtiers gathering in the galleries around him, approaching the emperor over the bridges. It is a strange, awkward design not seen in any Mughal building before or after.

Beyond this palace is an open, pillared pavilion which tradition says was the astrologer's seat. Predictions and the movements of the stars were taken seriously in Akbar's court. Right behind it is the one-roomed pavilion that many call *Ankh Michauli*, where the emperor is believed to have played blindman's buff with the harem ladies. It is a whimsical and appealing thought but it is hard to believe that a man of Akbar's majesty would indulge in

such a pastime. This room was probably part of the royal treasury. Against the walls are recesses with sliding stone slabs on top where coins and gems could be kept. A gallery around the room provided place for the guards to stand. The carved struts that support the roof have monsters carved at one end, the traditional Indian way to guard treasures. Also more probable is that Todar Mal, Akbar's finance minister, and not an astrologer, sat outside.

Panch Mahal is another structure one can imagine Akbar dreaming up. It is a fantastic creation, a tall pyramidal structure consisting of five open pavilions, each progressively smaller in size. The pavilions are supported by pillars with the lowest having eighty-four, the numbers gradually diminishing with each successive storey, the highest consisting of only a domed canopy supported by just four pillars. It is a surprisingly elegant and airy building and it is easy to imagine the emperor climbing up to the higher floors for some fresh air.

Across the Diwan-i-Khas is the two-storeyed palace that was Akbar's personal quarters, his Khwabgah, literally the Palace of Dreams. No chronicle of this time ever really tells us exactly how the palace was used so one must surmise from the names, and hearsay. Akbar may have used the rooms on the first floor as his bedroom and sitting room while meeting his inner council in the lower chambers. Chronicles describe how Akbar would stride out of his chambers and walk towards the Diwan-i-Khas surrounded by people. Monserrate writes, "It is hard to exaggerate how accessible he makes himself to all who wish to audience with him. For he creates an opportunity almost every day for any of the common people to see him and converse with him, and he endeavours to show himself pleasant spoken and affable rather than severe towards all who come to speak with him." The court "is always thronged with multitudes of men of every type," for Akbar "is specially remarkable for his love of keeping great crowds of people around him."

Another more contemplative and artistic side of the monarch is revealed by the large, square pool before his bedchamber called Anup Talao. Four narrow pathways over the water end in a square seat in the centre of the pool. It is said that Mian Tansen, Akbar's leading court singer, performed here for his monarch. The acoustics of the place are so perfect that Akbar in his first floor chamber would have been able to hear every phrase and nuance in Tansen's singing.

Beyond lay the forbidden area, the *haramsara* or royal seraglio. Here only men of the royal family were permitted. The two most interesting palaces here are those called Jodha Bai's palace and Birbal's palace. Jodha Bai's palace was used by Akbar's Hindu wives, the principal queen being the princess of Amber, Jodha Bai. It is a stately building with an inner courtyard surrounded by suites of rooms. The enlightened Akbar allowed his Hindu queens to perform their religious ceremonies and the courtyard may have been used for that purpose. The walls are decorated with delicate carvings and ornamental niches, perforated grills and tapering pillars. It is a very feminine interior that contrasts sharply with the plain and rather forbidding exterior. The carvings blend Persian and Indian motifs from nature – birds, flowers, vines and the tree of life. Abul Fazl, observing his craftsmen at work, wrote, "Clever workmen chisel it so skilfully as no turner could with wood."

The harem area has many other exquisitely designed apartments, like the Turkish Sultana's palace and Miriam's palace. About the Turkish Sultana's palace, Fergusson wrote, "It is one of the richest, the most beautiful and the most naturalistic of Akbar's buildings... It is impossible to conceive anything so picturesque in outline or any building carved

and ornamental to such an extent without the smallest approach to being overdone or in bad taste." The most ornamental building in the *haramsara* is what is apocryphally called Birbal's palace. Though Raja Birbal was Akbar's most valued friend, even then it is impossible to believe he would have been allowed to live in a palace that overlooked the harem. This double-storeyed, profusely carved building has two apartments and was probably used by the two seniormost ladies of the harem, Akbar's mother, Mariam Makani, and his aunt, Gulbadan Begum.

Among all the buildings of Akbar at Agra, Fatehpur Sikri still retains its sense of time and place. On its isolated hill, without the intrusion of people or any other habitat, it has stayed like a historical theatre faithfully recreating the splendour of the court of one of the greatest kings India has seen. In Fatehpur Sikri, Akbar has his best epitaph.

above: The Buland Darwaza as seen from inside the Jami Masjid, Fatehpur Sikri
previous page: The Buland Darwaza viewed from outside, Fatehpur Sikri

A Majestic Harmony

Jahangir's Agra

SIKANDRA

Jahangir's reign was in many ways a hiatus in the architectural chronicle of Agra. Unlike his father, he had little inclination to take on the challenge of vast architectural projects. His tastes were more akin to those of his great-grandfather, Babur. He loved nature, enjoyed observing flora and fauna, and took pleasure in planning gardens, like those he created in Kashmir with flowing water channels, fountains and pleasure pavilions. During Jahangir's reign, Agra saw little by way of building activity. The few structures that came up were because of the personal interest taken by Empress Nur Jahan, but for another glorious chapter in its history of architecture, Agra would have to wait for Shah Jahan.

In contrast to his father's taste for the grandiose, Jahangir was a miniaturist. His true passion, beyond wine and opium, lay in the art of miniature painting. The royal school of painters flourished under his patronage. For him the painters were not mere illustrators of manuscripts but artists and they were encouraged to make original nature studies and fine portraits. Jahangir's autobiography shows clearly where the emperor's real interests lay. In *Tuzuk-i-Jahangiri*, he often talks of the paintings that caught his eye, rarely making mention of buildings that received his royal attention.

Of course, architecture did not come to a standstill during Jahangir's reign. Akbar had begun his mausoleum, but when he died in 1605, it was only partially built, and as a loyal son Jahangir had to involve himself with the task of its completion. Three years after Akbar's death, Jahangir visited the site of the mausoleum at Sikandra and found that the work was progressing very slowly. As he writes, "When I entered, I saw no building over the tomb such as I would approve of, for I had expected to see an edifice which travellers would pronounce to be unrivalled in the world." The architects, he added, "went on building after their taste ... They had been three or four years at work, when I ordered clever architects ... to build up several parts as I had before directed, gradually a noble edifice arose and a splendid garden was laid out around the mausoleum."

Jahangir may have claimed to rescue the building at Sikandra but his actual contributions were probably merely cosmetic. The architects would have kept to the plan originally approved by Akbar, Jahangir's contribution being in the addition of marble which now topped the canopies and *chhatris*, the laying out of the 'splendid garden' and the marble cloisters on the top floor. Anyone familiar with his taste in building would recognise at Sikandra the unmistakable hand of Akbar. It is vigorously planned, primarily using red sandstone and, at times, is designed with a touch of royal whim.

Jahangir's reign was a period of transition between the majestic style of Akbar and the more opulent creations of his son, Shah Jahan. The tomb at Sikandra was completed in 1613, eight years after the death of Akbar. The building is placed in the centre of an extensive Mughal garden in the traditional *charbagh* style and is entered through an

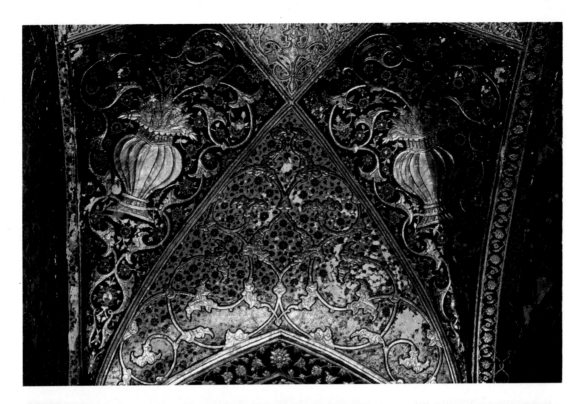

previous page: The gateway to Akbar's mausoleum, Sikandra, top: The ceilings of Sikandra were painted with patterns using Persian motifs, above: Details of ceiling decoration, Sikandra

impressive gateway in the southern perimeter wall. The gateway is a pleasing creation with carvings, mosaic and inlay work, and four slim minarets soaring at the four corners on top. This is the first time that minarets were used in this manner and would later give the Taj Mahal its airy elegance.

The tomb is reached through a garden bisected by broad, paved walks. The tomb itself has been visualised in a stepped, pyramidal form without a pinnacle. Like the Panch Mahal at Fatehpur Sikri, the five storeys of the building rise, diminishing in scale, the ground floor being pierced by a series of arches. An arcaded enclosure within contains Akbar's tomb. The first three storeys are in sandstone with a profusion of pillared arcades and kiosks with marble roofs. In sharp contrast, the top floor is in pristine white marble.

The top floor is an open, colonnaded enclosure with a view of the Yamuna river and, on clear days, the soaring minarets of the Taj Mahal in the misty distance. Akbar's cenotaph stands in the middle of the open courtyard, on a raised platform. On the cenotaph are carved the ninety names of Allah, in delicate calligraphy. The phrase *Allah hu Akbar, Jalla Jalaluhu* – God is great, Eminent in His glory – is inscribed on two faces of the marble cenotaph. The platform and the cenotaph are profusely carved with floral, arabesque and geometric motifs. There are also a few Chinese-style cloud forms and butterflies. A slender marble kiosk rises at each corner of this enclosure.

The building at Sikandra has no dome and Fergusson felt that the platform in the centre of the top floor was designed to support a chamber crowned with a light dome ... The platform is supported on massive piers which would have been quite strong enough to support a dome. The British traveller Finch, who visited Sikandra in 1611, says something similar. The tomb was meant "to be inarched over with the most curious white and speckled marble, and to be sealed all within with pure sheet-gold, richly inwrought." Instead, on a later visit he noticed over the upper floor "a rich tent, with a semaine over the tomb." The decision not to have a dome may have been Jahangir's, without too felicitous a result.

Looking at Sikandra as a whole, the vigour and power of the lower floors do not blend too well with the delicacy of the chaste snowy marble on top. Probably here too is evidence of Jahangir's hand, because Akbar never used marble as the main material of building, preferring it instead as a decorative element to embellish the carvings. Also, the flat upper floor gives the structure a strangely truncated look, a lack of harmony, as if the work was left incomplete.

However, taken individually, there are elements at Sikandra that are worth noticing. The plan and elevation through the storeys is rather unusual, and the ground floor by itself is built with grandeur. Sadly, it does not blend too well with the clusters of *chhatris*, which seem rather excessive, or with the top floor which, for all its delicately wrought design, looks oddly light and ephemeral.

ITMAD-UD-DAULA'S TOMB

Mirza Ghiyas Beg, a penniless Persian came to Akbar's court hoping to make a fortune and his rise in the Mughal court must have surprised even him. It was in the reign of Jahangir that his meteoric rise to power began and it is one of the most remarkable success stories of the time. What was even more amazing was the fact that he owed his eminence and the power and influence of his family through the reigns of two monarchs, to two women – his daughter Mehrunnissa, and his granddaughter Arjumand Bano. It was the advantageous marriages of these women that ultimately gave Ghiyas Beg the position of prime minister of the realm with the title of Itmad-ud-Daula (Reliance of the State).

It was Mehrunnissa who first married Emperor Jahangir, who bestowed on her the title of Nur Jahan and soon after left the keys of the kingdom in her hand. Then Arjumand Bano wed Prince Khurram who ascended the throne as Shah Jahan and bestowed the title Mumtaz Mahal on her. What was truly unique about both aunt and niece was that they were both favourites of their husbands and wielded enormous influence as royal consorts. Consequently, if anyone deserved a marble memorial, it was Mirza Ghiyas Beg, the Itmad-ud-Daula.

Nur Jahan built the mausoleum of her father in 1626, on the left bank of the river Yamuna. This is the first Mughal monument to be built completely in marble and in many ways it foreshadows the memorial that Mumtaz Mahal would get one day. Nur Jahan chose this site because a *baradari* or pleasure pavilion built by her father already stood there. Ghiyas Beg's wife Asmat Begum, who died first, was buried here before him and it is her grave that is in the centre of the room with Ghiyas Beg's tomb beside hers. The same layout is also to be seen at the Taj Mahal.

Itmad-ud-Daula's tomb stands in the middle of a garden in the traditional *charbagh* style, enclosed by a wall pierced with red sandstone gateways. The square building stands on a raised terrace with an octagonal turret in two stages, topped by a domed cupola. Coming upon it, a visitor is dazzled by its pristine whiteness and the luxurious decoration in fine pietra-dura inlays. In reality, the design of the structure itself is not remarkable. There is no impressive architectural plan, none of the vitality and exuberance of the carvings of Akbar's reign. It is, instead, a simple, slightly heavy box-like structure. What gives it its jewel-casket look and dazzles the eye is the decoration and the sheen of the marble, a reflection of the Persian wave prevalent through the royal court. During Jahangir's reign, sadly Akbar's efforts at creating a synthesis of Indian and Islamic styles was abandoned and the ornamental and ceremonial style came back into being.

The square pavilion is topped by a curving canopy placed in the middle of a terraced roof. There are four short corner towers that are a little heavy for the structure. The central room containing the cenotaph is surrounded by interconnecting rooms. Here the sunlight is filtered in softly through exquisitely carved lattice screens that have been described as 'gossamer of fretted grilles.' The pietra-dura work is of the finest quality, executed with gracefulness without being over-ornamental. The inlay is in coloured stone to balance the marble in a blend of honey, gold and black, with well harmonised geometrics and arabesques, a profusion of leaves and flowers, *guldasta*,

above: *Details of geometric inlay work, Itmad-ud-Daula's tomb*
previous page: *The tomb of Itmad-ud-Daula, built by Noorjahan*

flower vases, cups and decanters in a very Persian style. The overall covering of inlay work also gives the building a feminine character, reflecting the empress who built it. It is intimate in size, decorative and subtle in character, and charms the viewer without overwhelming him.

With the tomb of Itmad-ud-Daula, Akbari architecture vanished totally from Agra. Shah Jahan had always shown a preference for the decorative, where the ornamental cover of the building, the lattice screens, the pietra-dura inlays, the gold leaf ceilings took precedence over the actual design of the buildings. Akbar's architectural majesty was replaced by a taste for opulence that at times moved very close to mere prettiness. Which is probably why, after four centuries, it is the Akbari buildings that have retained their character with greater power. Fatehpur Sikri may not dazzle like the Taj Mahal, but it is finally a more impressive example of architecture.

above: *The graves of Itmad-ud-Daula and his wife*
facing page: *Details of the floral and geometric motifs painted on the ceiling, Itmad-ud-Daula's tomb*

A Melody in Marble

Shahjahan's Agra

THE TAJ MAHAL

Arjumand Bano was not destined to remain an empress for long. Married at twenty-one to Jahangir's third son, Prince Khurram, she had stayed loyally by his side through many upheavals. The prince had rebelled against his father and wandered across the kingdom as a fugitive, finally buying peace by sending two young sons to the royal court as hostages as guarantee for his good behaviour. He had ascended the throne after a bloody battle of succession, in 1628, taking upon himself the title of Shah Jahan. His beloved he showered with many titles, the most popular among them being Mumtaz Mahal (Exalted of the Palace) and Mumtaz-ul-Zamani (Distinguished of the Age). It seemed that finally she would live the life she had been preparing for, as the royal consort of the emperor of Hindustan.

In the fourth year of his reign, Shah Jahan went on an expedition to the South to quell

above: View of the Taj Mahal from the Jamuna River
following page: Two views of the red sandstone
gateway of the Taj Mahal. (left) from the outside,
(right) inside, facing the Taj Mahal

a rebellion and as was her wont, Mumtaz Mahal accompanied him. At Burhanpur, in June 1631, she died at childbirth. In all, she bore fourteen children, four sons and three daughters of whom survived her. When Arjumand Bano died, she was only thirty-nine.

Shah Jahan was inconsolable and the chronicles of the time tell of how for two years the royal court was in mourning. There was no music, no feasting, and no celebrations of any kind. It was at this time that the monarch decided to build a memorial to his queen that the world would never forget. Shah Jahan, the most energetic and ambitious builder among the Mughals, conceived of a poem in marble where Arjumand Bano Begum would sleep forever.

Mumtaz's body was temporarily buried in the Zainabad garden at Burhanpur. Six months later it was brought to Agra accompanied by her son Shah Shuja, and her close companion and lady-in-waiting, Sati-un-nissa Khanum. The site selected for her final resting place was in a garden by the Yamuna River that was not marked by any other structure nearby. The garden had originally been laid by Raja Man Singh of Amber and now belonged to his grandson, Raja Jai Singh. By a royal *farman*, Shah Jahan gave Jai Singh four *havelis* in exchange for the garden. The site was also chosen because it was a

bend in the river and could be viewed from Shah Jahan's personal rooms in the palaces of Agra Fort.

The work on the memorial began in the fifth year of Shah Jahan's reign and many craftsmen and calligraphers, stone carvers and building specialists came from lands as distant as Persia and Turkey. Twenty thousand workers laboured for seventeen years to build the memorial that posterity came to know as the Taj Mahal. In its marble serenity, perfect proportions, grace and majesty, this superb mausoleum is a befitting memorial to the beautiful Arjumand Bano. Three decades later, in 1666, Shah Jahan would be laid to rest beside her.

For centuries the Taj Mahal has inspired poets and writers, painters and musicians. Few who have come to Agra to see it have gone away untouched by it. For some it is a testimony of a monarch's love for his queen; for others it is a symbol of a Mughal's swelling arrogance and ambition. Perhaps, it is both. Shah Jahan loved his wife deeply, but he also did not miss the opportunity to build an extravagant memorial as a symbol of his power and majesty. Still, somewhere in the Taj Mahal's marble corridors wanders the gentle shadow of a woman who died too young. The poet Rabindranath Tagore paid his

tribute to the mausoleum thus:

Through emeralds, rubies, pearls are all
But as glitter of a rainbow tricking out empty air
And must pass away
Yet still one solitary tear
Would hang on the cheek of time
In the form of this white and gleaming Taj Mahal.

The Taj Mahal reveals itself to the viewer with the dramatic power of visual theatre. Near the main gate in the south, it looms above in marble and sandstone, with inlaid flowers and intricate calligraphy around the archway, *chhatris* soaring above. The octagonal chamber within is dark, and light streams in from the opposite doorway. Here, framed by the arch of the doorway like a curtain rising, the snowy marble glittering against a blue sky, is the Taj Mahal.

A pathway runs through the precisely laid Mughal garden, past the water channel in the centre, the rows of fountains, the square pool halfway down the path with its reflection of the Taj Mahal in the water. The marble mausoleum stands at the end of the path, surprisingly powerful in its majesty, awaiting humble obeisance, like a monarch. The octagonal walls leading up to a dome piercing the sky, the four elegant, slim minarets at the four corners of the plinth framing it – like a stage, the tomb is set at one end of the garden and not in the centre, as was the earlier tradition. It stands framed against the sky with the river below, the setting of the sandstone mosque and its *jawab* (an identical mosque where no prayers are offered since it faces away from the Mecca) at the west and east balancing and framing the picture.

Like true dramatists, the Taj's creators have used the ever-changing moods of nature to give their creation a setting that is never the same. During the day the colour of the sky moves from soft shell pink at dawn to a deeper blue in the daytime, the sun a relentless light without shadows at noon, and the marble a soft, pearly white at the beginning of the day turning a glittering crystal. In the evening the amber of the sky adds shadows and a mysterious touch of gold to the dome and minarets, and at night by the gentle silver rays of the moon, the Taj Mahal seems to float away like an ethereal dream.

Let us also not forget the seasons. The Taj Mahal mirrors every change of the seasons. When the clouds gather in the sky around it and the blowing wind bends the trees in the garden, the Taj also has a moody blue tint in its marble. It vanishes and appears in the dawn mists of winter, like a drifting mirage across the still waters of the Yamuna. In the summer heat, it raises a serene face to the sky, welcoming you across the garden to its dim, cool interiors. And in the monsoons it stands washed in lashing rain with lightning flickering behind it. It can be solid and earthbound, airy and fragile. White, amber, grey and gold – the many faces of the Taj Mahal are the theatre of architecture at its best.

Finally, for all its overwhelming external beauty, it still carries its store of tragedy within where the two graves lie. You cannot forget that this is a mausoleum, built out of grief at the death of a young woman. Inside, the actual graves of Shah Jahan and Mumtaz Mahal are in an underground vault. Directly above it is the octagonal chamber where the two cenotaphs lie. As was traditionally done, the empress' body lies in the exact centre. In 1666, Shah Jahan's coffin was brought by river and laid beside her. It is hard

to believe that he had wished to build another mausoleum for himself across the river in black marble, as has been suggested by some art-historians. Firstly, there is no physical evidence either in archaeological remains or in any mentions in the chronicles of the time. Then, it is easier to believe that, as they had done during their lifetime, the monarch and his empress would prefer to be together even in death.

In the words of Sir Edwin Arnold:

Not architecture! as all others are
But the proud passion of an Emperor's love
Wrought into living stone, which gleams and soars
With body and beauty shrinking soul and thought

For centuries there has been a running controversy about the architect of the Taj Mahal.

previous page: One of the greatest architectural masterpieces in the world, the incomparable Taj Mahal
facing page: The richly decorated walls with pilasters and the subsidiary domes are in perfect harmony with the central structure
above: Lady at the entrance gate on the left dwarfed by the huge minarets of Taj Mahal
following page: Entrance to the cenotaph room, Taj Mahal

Countries from Persia and Turkey to France and Italy have laid claims to the honour. Shah Jahan gathered the best talents from many lands for the job, it is true, but no mention is made anywhere of an architect. The craftsmen, masons and labourers were placed under the supervision of two noblemen, Mir Abdul Karim and Makramat Khan.

No contemporary writer mentions the name of a principal designer for the Taj Mahal. The only name that crops up is that of Ustad Ahmad Lahori, as its Mimar-i-Kul or chief architect, a traditional supervisory post. An inscription on his grave at Aurangabad says that he was the builder of the Taj Mahal and the Jami Masjid at Delhi. This is confirmed in the writing of his eldest son, Ataullah Rashidi, and a *masnavi* (rhyming couplets having profound spiritual meaning) written by another son, Lutfullah, in 1656, when Shah Jahan was still emperor.

The usual practise with Shah Jahan was to have a team of architects present their designs to him and a final version be created out of the elements approved by the emperor. A wooden model was then made under the supervision of the Mimar-i-Kul. In such a joint enterprise, the contribution of Shah Jahan himself cannot be dismissed. He possessed an aesthetic mind and much more than any architect, it was his personal taste that gave his buildings their character. Finally, one has to remember that the Taj Mahal is the final result of centuries of Mughal designs of tombs. From Humayun's tomb to Sikandra and Itmad-ud-Daula's tomb, there were elements that were taken and refined for the Taj Mahal.

Shah Jahan's other passion, apart from architecture, was the collection and designing of jewellery. He was an excellent judge of precious stones, and miniature paintings of the period show him wearing a lot of jewellery and holding up a turban ornament-like piece in his hand. He said his prayers using a perfect set of pearls as prayer beads. He built the Peacock Throne and had it encrusted with jewels. There is also the tale of how, when Aurangzeb asked his imprisoned father for some jewels, Shah Jahan flew into a rage and threatened to grind them into powder before he let his son use them. In the Taj Mahal, he visualised a building in marble and then decorated it with inlay in semi-precious stones with the fineness of crafted jewellery.

Europeans tried hard to lay claims to the creation of the Taj Mahal and the myth that took the longest to die was the story begun by Father Manrique who, after a visit to Agra in 1640, proclaimed that the Taj Mahal was designed by the Venetian, Geronimo Veroneo. A jeweller by profession, Veroneo died in Lahore the same year and was buried in Agra. His gravestone, however, makes no mention of the Taj Mahal. There is no support for this fanciful story from any of the European travellers such as Peter Mundy or Jean Baptiste Tavernier, who were in Agra during the years when the Taj Mahal was built. They were both meticulous chroniclers and would hardly have failed to mention such a momentous fact as a European designer of the Taj. Veroneo, in any case, was a jeweller who couldn't possibly have possessed the expertise to plan a structure as intricately fashioned as the Taj Mahal.

Another name that came up often was that of Isa Muhammad Effendi, an architect supposedly sent by the Sultan of Turkey. This claim was made centuries later in a Persian manuscript written in 1878, by Mughal Beg. Again, there is no support from contemporary chroniclers, and though Beg claims his writing is based on earlier works, he fails conveniently to mention their names.

Some British writers in the late nineteenth century came up with the name of a

above: *Details of marble carved jali screen, Taj Mahal*
facing page: *Details of marble inlay work, Taj Mahal*
following page: *Marble cenotaphs of Mumtaz Mahal and Shahjahan*

Frenchman, Austin de Bordeaux. Austin, again a jeweller making a precarious living off his wits in Agra, died in 1632, even before work on the Taj Mahal had begun. What these Western writers failed to understand was that Shah Jahan and other Mughals, like Akbar, were evolved builders themselves with very clear ideas of what they wanted to build. They hired specialists in the different areas of building work, but the building itself was always a creation they inspired. If there was a chief architect of the Taj Mahal, it was Shah Jahan himself.

Among the experts he called upon, many are mentioned by name in the records with details of their monthly salaries. There was the famous calligrapher Amanat Khan Shirazi, whose name appears at the end of an inscription at the entrance of the tomb. Ismail Khan Afandi built the two-shell dome. The master mason, Muhammad Hanif was from Baghdad and Kayam Khan, a pinnacle-maker, came from Lahore. Chiranjilal, sculptor and mosaicist, and Jamnadas, an inlayer, were from Delhi, while another sculptor, Baldeodas, came from Multan. Their salaries, in the mid-seventeenth century, ranged from four hundred to a thousand rupees a month. The water channel system in the garden was probably the work of Ali Mardan Khan, who would later bring the waters of the Yamuna into Shahjahanabad in Delhi, through a canal.

The royal treasury provided forty thousand *tolas* (four hundred and sixty kilos) of pure gold and, of course, the cash to pay the salaries. The material for the building was then gathered: the purest white marble from Makrana in Rajasthan; crystal from China; lapis lazuli and sapphires from Lanka; jasper from Punjab; carnelian from Baghdad; turquoise from Tibet; Yemen sent agates; the corals came from Arabia and the Red Sea; the garnets were from Bundelkhand; the diamonds from Jaisalmer; and onyx and amethyst from Persia; European chalcedony and sandstone from Sikri; also, there was jade, mother-of-pearl, topaz, emeralds, rubies ....

The forecourt of the Taj complex has the crypts of Mumtaz Mahal's close companions, Sati-un-nissa Khanum and Fatehpuri Begum. Here too are the graves of two other queens of Shah Jahan, Sarhindi Begum and Akbarabadi Begum. The forecourt also has the Jilau Khana or a bazaar with cloisters, and leads to the main entrance of the tomb. This imposing gateway has been built in sandstone and marble with octagonal kiosks on top and eleven *chhatris* with marble cupolas, and flanked by pinnacles. An imposing structure thirty metres high, it is a fitting entrance portal to the Taj Mahal.

Beyond, at the end of the *charbagh* garden and pathway, the mausoleum stands on a marble plinth six metre high with four minarets at each corner, beautifully flanking the central structure. The marble plinth stands on a high sandstone platform, and at two ends of the base are two identical sandstone structures – a mosque on the west and the Mehman Khana (guest house) on the east – helping to focus the viewer's eye on the marble structure in the middle.

Like earlier Mughal mausoleums, the main tomb is octagonal in plan and twenty-five metres in height. The mortuary hall within is decorated with masterly inlay and dado panels in high relief. The bulbous double dome rises to a total height of forty-five metres, making it tower over the structure. With four *chhatris* flanking and balancing the high drum that gives it the requisite height, the Taj Mahal rises to a total height of nearly seventy-five metres.

The two cenotaphs in the centre of the mortuary hall are surrounded by a marble screen, which is a marvel of carving with the texture of lace. It is said that initially there was a solid gold, jewel-encrusted railing enclosing the cenotaph but Shah Jahan had it removed as

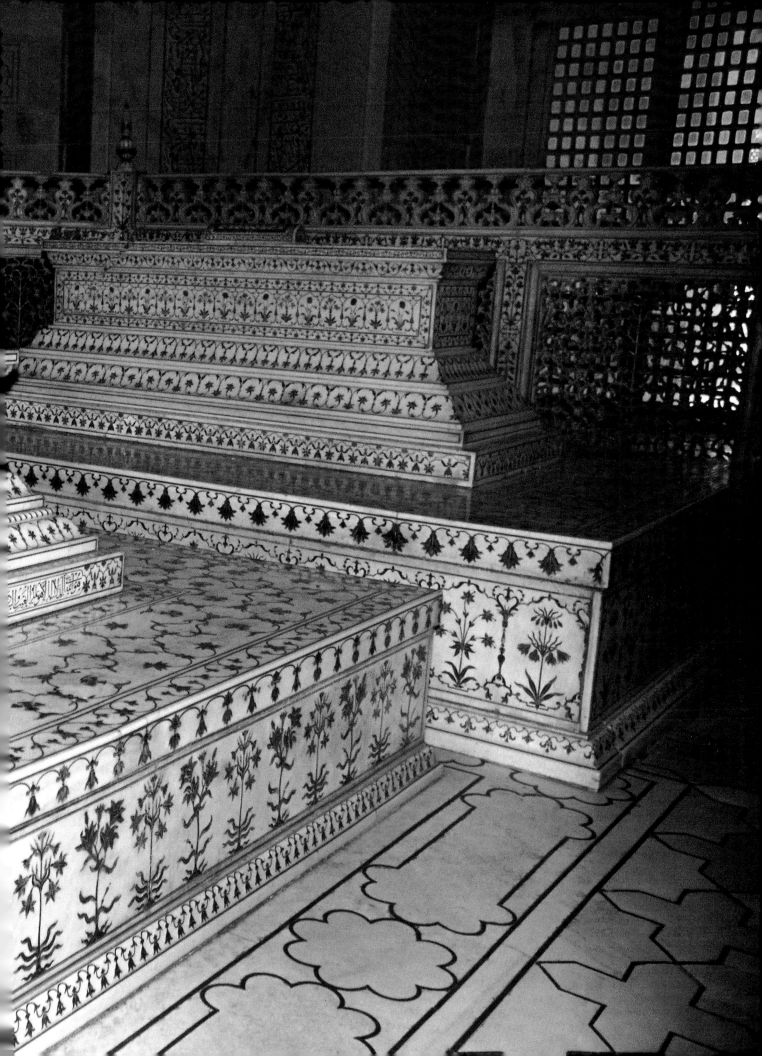

top: View of the cenotaphs, as seen from the upper gallery
above: The cenotaph is surrounded by an intricately carved marble screen, **facing page:** The entrance to the tomb, the inlay work used forty three varieties of semi-precious stones
following page: Details of pietra-dura work in traditional Indian floral motifs,
page no. 94-95: View of the Taj Mahal downstream from the Jamuna. As seen from the Bangla Pavilion, Agra Fort

he feared it would be spoiled by vandals. Two storeys of eight rooms surround the central chamber. The light falls softly over the cenotaph through the *jali* screen on the windows of these two floors as they are fitted with opaque glass.

A closer look at the finer details of the building will bring to light the fine inlay with delicately balanced panels of floral, arabesque and geometric designs. Many of these designs are inspired by the floral borders of miniature paintings, which were done in the time of Jahangir. The craftsmanship is so fine, it is impossible to find the joints in the inlay where at times the artist used as many as forty-eight tiny pieces of semi-precious stone in the petals of a single flower. Framing the archways are panels in black-and-white calligraphy of the verses from the *Quran*, and some of the finest calligraphy can be seen on the two headstones.

Every dusk, in the rays of the setting sun the marble dome turns golden. As the first cluster of stars appears in the sky behind it, the day bids adieu to a creation that transcends any other on earth in its ethereal perfection.

Views of the lively bazaars of modern Agra. Once the elegant capital city of the Mughals, today Agra is like most other towns of North India. Only the monuments remind the visitor of its magnificent past